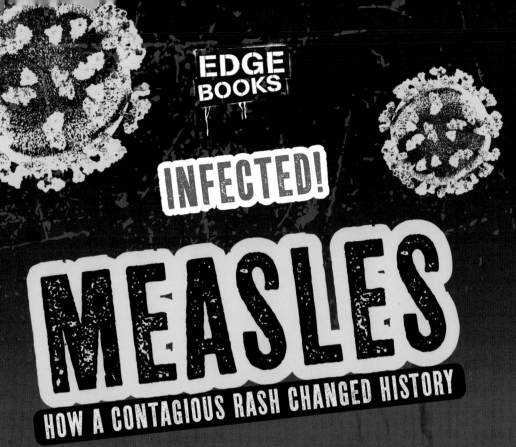

EDGE
BOOKS™

INFECTED!

MEASLES

HOW A CONTAGIOUS RASH CHANGED HISTORY

by Mark L. Lewis

Consultant

David N. Fisman, MD
Professor, Dalla Lana School of Public Health
University of Toronto

CAPSTONE PRESS
a capstone imprint

Edge Books are published by Capstone Press,
1710 Roe Crest Drive, North Mankato, Minnesota 56003
www.mycapstone.com

Library of Congress Cataloging-in-Publication Data
Names: Lewis, Mark L., 1991- author.
Title: Measles : how a contagious rash changed history / Mark L. Lewis.
Description: North Mankato, Minnesota : Capstone Press, [2020] | Series: Infected! | Audience: Grades 4 to 6. | Includes bibliographical references and index.
Identifiers: LCCN 2018061090 (print) | LCCN 2019004500 (ebook) | ISBN 9781543572445 (ebook) | ISBN 9781543572407 (hardcover)
Subjects: LCSH: Measles--Juvenile literature. | Measles--History--Juvenile literature. | Epidemics--History--Juvenile literature. | Diseases and history--Juvenile literature.
Classification: LCC RA644.M5 (ebook) | LCC RA644.M5 L485 2020 (print) | DDC 614.5/23--dc23
LC record available at https://lccn.loc.gov/2018061090

All internet sites appearing in back matter were available and accurate when this book was sent to press.

Editorial Credits
Editor: Megan Ellis
Designer: Craig Hinton
Production Specialist: Craig Hinton

Photo Credits
Alamy: The History Collection, 19; AP Images: Diego Diaz/Icon Sportswire, 29, Gillian Flaccus, 27, Mike Hutmacher/The Wichita Eagle, 23; Centers for Disease Control and Prevention: Alan Janssen/Public Health Image Library, 14–15, Alison M. Maiuri/Public Health Image Library, cover (top), 1, Carlos Alonso/Public Health Image Library, 25, Public Health Image Library, 13; iStockphoto: Dr_Microbe, 8, Fat Camera, cover (bottom); North Wind Picture Archives: 16; Red Line Editorial: 26; Science Source: Lowell Georgia, 11, P. Marazzi, 9, Science Source, 12; Shutterstock Images: Africa Studio, 5, Andrey_Popov, 21, Yusnizam Yusof, 6

Design Elements
Shutterstock Images

Printed in the United States of America.
112019   000110

TABLE OF CONTENTS

CHAPTER 1

THE RETURN OF MEASLES

Silvia Rosetti lives in Rome. In 2017 she was 32 weeks pregnant. She had a smooth pregnancy until she got sick. The symptoms developed quickly. Rosetti had a fever and a cough. She was congested. She could not breathe. She needed to go to the hospital.

When she arrived, the doctors told her she had measles. She was never **vaccinated** as a child. This meant she did not receive the measles **vaccine**. The doctors performed a surgery to deliver her son eight weeks early. Doctors **isolated** Rosetti and her son away from each other and other infants. They had to make sure her child was not infected.

vaccinate—to give someone a shot of medicine that prevents disease
vaccine—a substance made up of dead, weakened, or living organisms that is given to a person to protect against a disease
isolate—to keep apart from a group so that an illness does not spread

Rosetti spent five days in the hospital. Her illness caused a rash on her eyes. She could not see. She also developed pneumonia. It is an infection that affects the lungs. During this time, she was not able to see her son. She had to wait until her symptoms were gone.

Rosetti recovered from her illness, and her son is healthy. But measles is a dangerous and highly contagious disease. It is making a comeback.

FAST FACT

A three-week-old infant contracted measles from his mother in Israel in 2018. He became the youngest person on record to be infected with measles.

Pregnancy increases a person's risk for contracting measles.

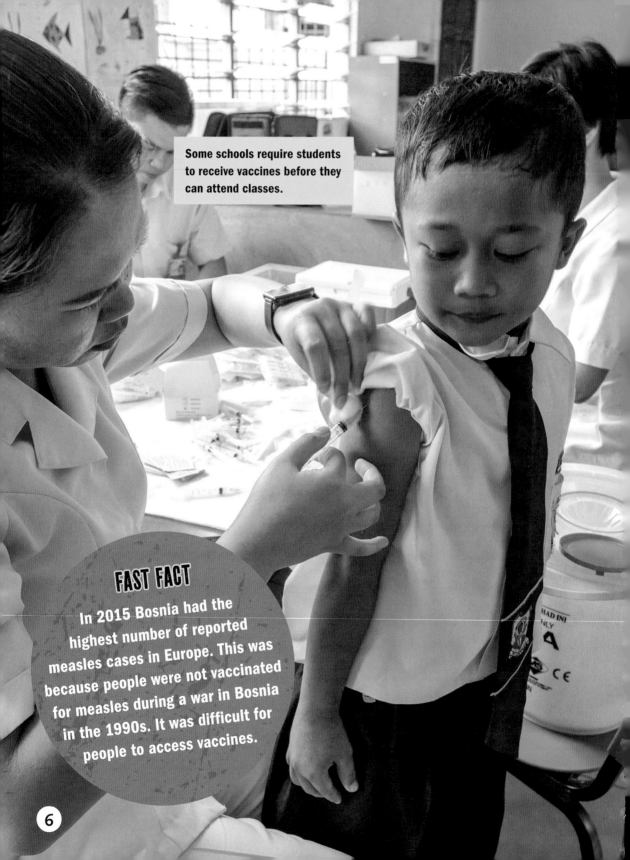

Some schools require students to receive vaccines before they can attend classes.

FAST FACT

In 2015 Bosnia had the highest number of reported measles cases in Europe. This was because people were not vaccinated for measles during a war in Bosnia in the 1990s. It was difficult for people to access vaccines.

A RISE IN MEASLES CASES

Measles is a preventable disease. However, some people do not get vaccinated. This puts them at risk for contracting measles. Other people around them may also contract measles. They may not be old enough to receive the vaccines. They may also have **immune systems** that are **compromised**.

Measles diagnoses are rising in many countries. Countries throughout Europe experienced a spike in measles diagnoses in the 2010s. In 2010 European cases rose from 7,000 to more than 30,000. In 2011 it was 33,000. This spike came after vaccination rates fell to a 10-year low in 2004. Italy, Greece, France, Romania, and Ukraine were hit especially hard in 2017. These countries did not require children to be vaccinated for measles.

Recent outbreaks caused some lawmakers to want change. Some politicians and parents are calling for vaccinations to be required for children in order to attend public schools.

immune system—the part of the body that fights infections
compromised—not functioning at full ability

CHAPTER **2**

WHAT CAUSES MEASLES?

Measles is a highly contagious virus. It spreads through the air. When someone with measles coughs, tiny droplets of infected spit enter the air. People breathe in that air. The tiny droplets can also land on hard surfaces, such as tables and doorknobs. The virus can live for up to two hours on hard surfaces. Without vaccination a person has a 90 percent chance of contracting measles if exposed.

The virus that causes measles is *Measles morbillivirus*.

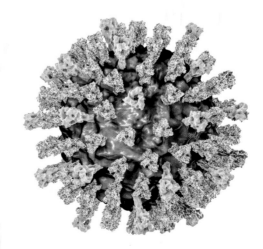

Koplik spots

SYMPTOMS

Symptoms usually begin one to two weeks after contracting the virus. The first symptoms are fever and cough. Patients develop a runny nose and red, watery eyes.

After two days of fever and cough, patients start getting a rash. White spots appear on the inside of the mouth first. Then a rash spreads over the rest of the body. It starts near the face. The rash then moves down the neck, chest, arms, and legs.

Rashes can cover most of the patient's body. The red splotches might run together. Then the fever gets worse. A person's temperature may rise to more than 104 degrees Fahrenheit (40 degrees Celsius). A patient with measles begins to recover after a week. The fever goes down. The rash disappears slowly.

COMPLICATIONS

The rash and fever do not make measles deadly. But measles causes many dangerous complications, or secondary illnesses. Most measles deaths are caused by complications, not the disease itself.

The most common complications are ear infections. Even though ear infections are common, they are still dangerous. Patients may have permanent hearing loss after contracting measles.

One report estimates that measles causes 60,000 cases of blindness every year. A patient's eye can become scarred. With a scarred eye, a person is no longer able to see.

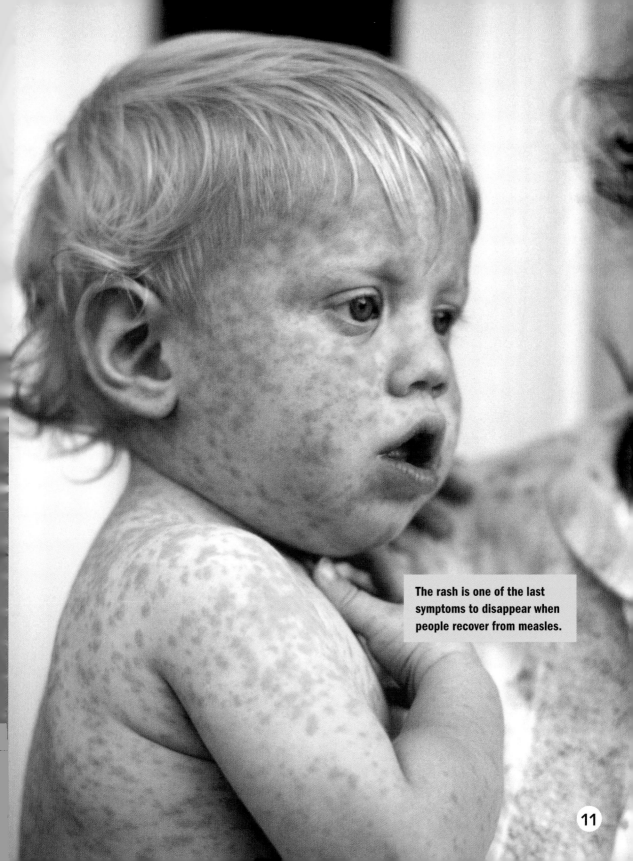

The rash is one of the last symptoms to disappear when people recover from measles.

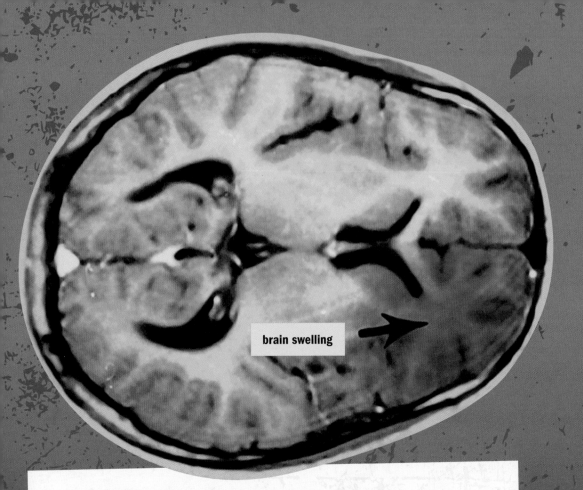

brain swelling

Measles causes some patients' brains to swell. This is called encephalitis. It is very dangerous. Patients can suffer brain damage. They may also have hearing loss. They may even die.

Pneumonia is another serious complication. Pneumonia is an infection in the lungs. According to the Centers for Disease Control and Prevention (CDC), pneumonia is the most common cause of death for children with measles complications.

People who are malnourished may have a higher risk of developing measles complications. Someone who is malnourished does not get enough food or nutrients. They may not get enough vitamin A in their diet. Vitamin A helps the body fight infections. It also helps the eyes, heart, lungs, and kidneys.

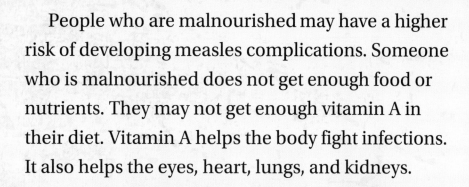

FAST FACT

Some vegetables that are good sources of vitamin A are carrots, broccoli, sweet potatoes, and squash. Dairy products such as eggs and milk are also good sources of vitamin A.

Measles patients who are malnourished may have weaker immune systems due to a lack of vitamin A.

CHAPTER 3

THE HISTORY OF MEASLES

Measles is an ancient disease. Doctors in Asia and northern Africa knew about measles as early as the AD 400s. Rhazes, a Persian doctor, published the first widespread diagnosis of measles in 900. Historians believe measles could have originated in animals. The virus resembles rinderpest. It is a virus that used to affect cows.

MEASLES EPIDEMICS

Measles **epidemics** have been common throughout history. They come in waves. Epidemics usually occur every two to three years.

epidemic—an outbreak of a disease that affects many people within a particular region

Public health workers travel to places with measles epidemics. They provide vaccines and other medicine.

FAST FACT

Humans are the only reservoir for measles. This means the measles virus can live in humans' bodies, but not in the bodies of animals.

Measles outbreaks have caused many deaths in Europe and Asia since ancient times. The worst epidemics occurred because of **colonization**. Researchers believe that in 1492 Christopher Columbus was the first European person to bring measles to the Americas. Measles had a 25 percent mortality rate in North America during colonization.

European settlers traded goods with Native Americans. This led to the spread of disease.

colonization—the process by which European settlers came to North and South America

THE SPREAD OF DISEASES

European settlers brought many diseases to North America, including measles and smallpox. These diseases had high mortality rates. Scientists estimate that 95 percent of native populations in North America died in the first 150 years of European colonization due to diseases from European settlers.

People native to North and Central America had never been exposed to measles. They were not **immune** to the illness. European settlers probably did not know that they carried diseases across the ocean. The settlers were naturally more resistant to measles after generations of being exposed to the disease. Additionally some people with measles do not show symptoms for a few days. They can pass the disease to other people.

FAST FACT

More Native American deaths were caused by European diseases than by any weapon.

immune—unable to contract a certain illness

CHAPTER 4

INFECTIONS AND VACCINES

Measles was a widespread and deadly disease. Before scientists created a vaccine, measles caused 2.6 million deaths every year. Most of those who died were children under 5 years old. Children have less developed immune systems than adults. Their bodies have a hard time fighting the virus.

People did not know what caused measles. They also did not know how to treat it. Before the 1700s, a common treatment for measles was **bloodletting**. Doctors would remove some of the patient's blood.

bloodletting—an ancient medical practice in which doctors cut a person's vein so "bad" blood would leave the body

In 1757 Scottish doctor Francis Home proved that something contagious caused measles. He tried to make a measles vaccine. But he did not know enough about measles. The vaccine did not work. In the mid-1900s, scientists began developing a working measles vaccine.

Francis Home lived from 1719 to 1813.

DEVELOPING THE VACCINE

In the 1950s Dr. Samuel Katz began creating a vaccine. Katz had a **hypothesis** that a weakened version of the measles virus could be used to prevent a full measles infection. He knew that people who had contracted measles were immune to the disease later in life. Virus **antibodies** still lived in their bodies.

Katz finished a version of a vaccine in 1958. He tested it on himself. Then he tested his vaccine on children at a school in Boston, Massachusetts. He asked the parents for permission.

Katz's vaccine seemed to work. Children at the school developed measles antibodies. However, they also developed a mild form of measles. Katz needed to weaken the measles virus even further.

Katz was not the only one working on a vaccine. He worked in a lab with John F. Enders and Thomas C. Peebles. In 1954 Enders and Peebles collected blood samples from children with measles.

hypothesis—an educated guess about the outcome of an experiment
antibody—a cell that fights off infection

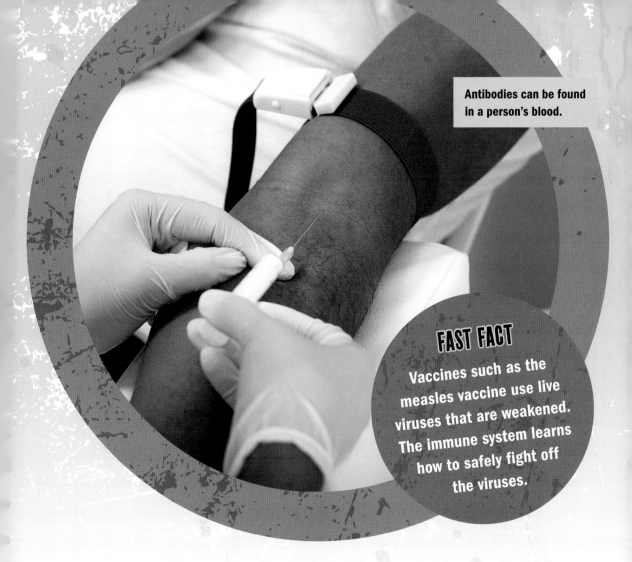

Antibodies can be found in a person's blood.

FAST FACT

Vaccines such as the measles vaccine use live viruses that are weakened. The immune system learns how to safely fight off the viruses.

The scientists took a sample of the virus from the blood of 13-year-old David Edmonston. They used this sample to create a vaccine.

In 1963 Katz, Enders, and Peebles created an effective vaccine. But other scientists thought it could be improved. In 1968 scientist Maurice Hilleman developed a better vaccine.

The CDC saw how effective the vaccine was right away. In 1978 the CDC set a goal to get rid of measles before 1982. Even though they did not meet their goal, measles infections were drastically reduced.

MEASLES VACCINE TODAY

Today children get multiple vaccines in one shot. The measles vaccine is usually combined with two or three other vaccines. The MMR vaccine protects against measles, mumps, and rubella. The MMRV vaccine protects against measles, mumps, rubella, and varicella. Varicella is the name of the virus that causes chicken pox.

Doctors give both the MMR and MMRV vaccines in two doses. The first one happens when a child is 12 to 15 months old. The second, a booster shot, is usually given when a child is 4 to 6 years old.

FAST FACT

The MMR vaccine is 97 percent effective when a child receives both doses. It is only 93 percent effective if a child just receives one dose.

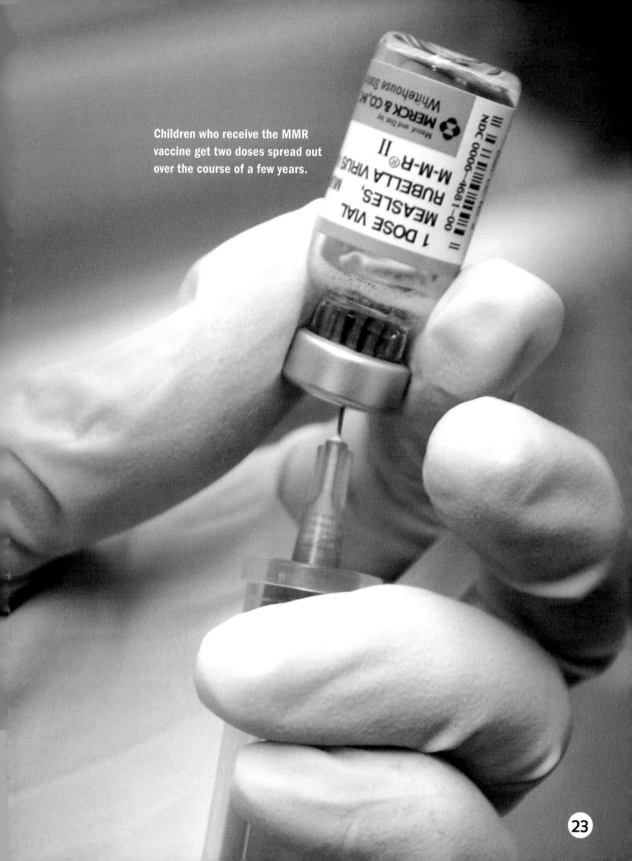

Children who receive the MMR vaccine get two doses spread out over the course of a few years.

CHAPTER 5

MEASLES TODAY

The World Health Organization (WHO) declared the United States free of measles in 2000. Britain was declared free of measles in 2016. From 2000 to 2016 the rate of measles infections worldwide dropped by 84 percent. However, after the disease was almost **eradicated**, measles diagnoses increased in both 2017 and 2018. In 2017 worldwide measles cases increased by 31 percent. This is due to a decrease in vaccination rates.

WORLDWIDE MEASLES INFECTIONS

Seventy percent of worldwide measles deaths in 2013 occurred in only six countries. These countries were the Democratic Republic of the Congo, Ethiopia, India, Indonesia, Nigeria, and Pakistan. These countries only have 28 percent of the global population. But more than 60 percent of children in these countries were not vaccinated against measles.

eradicate—to completely eliminate something

HERD IMMUNITY

Vaccines are different from other types of medication. They protect not only the vaccinated person but also other people who come into contact with that person. Medical workers are concerned about how the decrease in vaccination rates will affect herd immunity. Herd immunity is when a population is immune to a disease because the majority of that population is vaccinated.

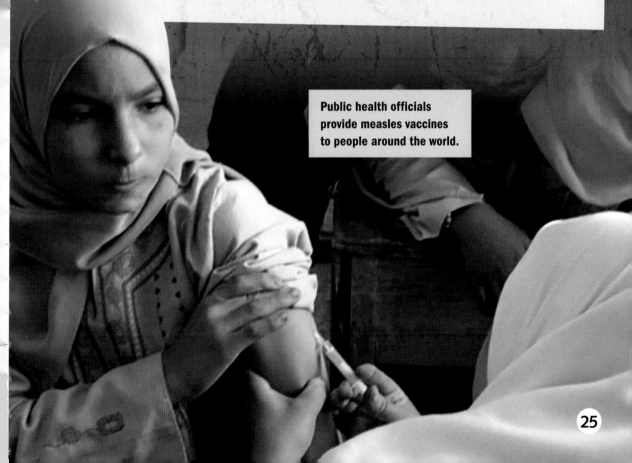

Public health officials provide measles vaccines to people around the world.

Herd immunity protects the entire population, even though each person is not immune to the disease. Some people have compromised immune systems. They could be born with weakened immune systems. They may have cancer or other diseases that attack their immune systems. These people can still become infected with measles.

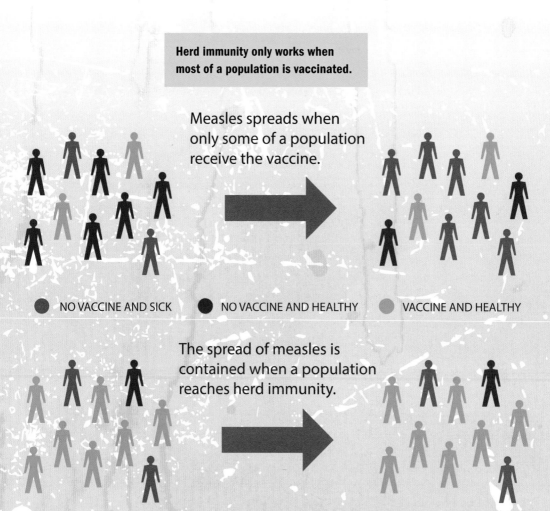

Herd immunity only works when most of a population is vaccinated.

Measles spreads when only some of a population receive the vaccine.

NO VACCINE AND SICK   NO VACCINE AND HEALTHY   VACCINE AND HEALTHY

The spread of measles is contained when a population reaches herd immunity.

MEASLES ALERT

STOP

ATTENTION ALL PATIENTS AND VISITORS
FOR YOUR PROTECTION

Please put on a MASK if:
· You are not immunized against measles
· You have had recent measles exposure
· You have any measles symptoms:
  - Runny nose   - Rash
  - Cough   - Fever

During a 2019 measles outbreak in Washington, businesses posted signs asking customers to wear masks if they felt sick.

Measles spreads easily. It is hard to reach the herd immunity **threshold** for measles. Scientists estimate that at least 95 percent of a population needs to be vaccinated against measles for the whole community to be safe. When vaccination rates drop below 95 percent, young children and people who are already sick are put at risk.

Illnesses such as measles return when too many people rely on herd immunity. These people may be hard to convince to get vaccines. They think that measles is gone forever so they do not need the vaccine. However, measles will only be eradicated if people keep receiving the vaccine.

threshold—the level that needs to be reached

MYTHS ABOUT MEASLES

Some people are choosing not to vaccinate their children. In 1998 a doctor published an article about vaccinations in a medical journal. The doctor claimed that vaccinations could cause autism in children. That article was proven false. However, many people use this article and other misleading science as evidence that they should not vaccinate their children.

Other people believe that measles is not a serious illness. Because measles is so common for unvaccinated people, parents believe that the illness is not dangerous. However, measles can have many complications.

There are no treatments to cure measles once symptoms appear. Scientists warn that low vaccination rates could lead to serious measles outbreaks. Between January 1, 2019, and March 1, 2019, there were 71 identified measles cases in Clark County, Washington. At the time, the county's MMR vaccination rate was only 81 percent.

Scientists believe that measles can be eradicated with vaccines. A related disease that affects cows, rinderpest, has been eradicated. This gives scientists hope for measles vaccines. However, herd immunity for measles must be reached to contain the spread of the disease.

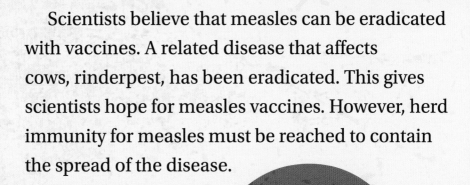

FAST FACT

In 2014, 110 visitors to Disneyland in Anaheim, California, contracted measles.

People who support vaccines participate in the March for Science in 2017.

GLOSSARY

antibody (AN-tih-boh-dee)—a cell that fights off infections

bloodletting (BLOOD-leh-ting)—an ancient medical practice in which doctors cut a person's vein so "bad" blood would leave the body

colonization (CAH-low-nie-zay-shuhn)—the process by which European settlers came to North and South America

compromised (COM-pro-mised)—not functioning at full ability

epidemic (eh-pih-DEH-mik)—an outbreak of a disease that affects many people within a particular region

eradicate (eh-RAH-dih-kate)—to completely eliminate something

hypothesis (hi-PAH-thih-sis)—an educated guess about the outcome of an experiment

immune (ih-MEWN)—unable to contract a certain illness

immune system (ih-MEWN SIS-tum)—the part of the body that fights infections

isolate (EYE-soh-late)—to keep apart from a group so that an illness does not spread

threshold (THRESH-hold)—the level that needs to be reached

vaccinate (VACK-sih-nate)—to give someone a shot of medicine that prevents disease

vaccine (vak-SEEN)—a substance made up of dead, weakened, or living organisms that is given to a person to protect against a disease

READ MORE

Alexander, Lori. *All in a Drop: How Antony Van Leeuwenhoek Discovered an Invisible World.* Boston: Houghton Mifflin Harcourt, 2018.

Cummings, Judy Dodge. *Epidemics and Pandemics: Real Tales of Deadly Diseases.* Mystery & Mayhem. White River Junction, Vt.: Nomad Press, 2018.

Gallagher, Amy. *Microbes.* London, UK: ThunderStone, 2017.

INTERNET SITES

KidsHealth: Measles
https://kidshealth.org/en/parents/measles.html

Science News for Students: 10 Things to Know About Measles
https://www.sciencenewsforstudents.org/article/
10-things-know-about-measles

TeensHealth: Immunizations
https://kidshealth.org/en/teens/immunizations.html

INDEX